minimalist
spaces

Conception: Arian Mostaedi
Publishers: Carles Broto & Josep Mª Minguet
Architecture Adviser: Pilar Chueca
Graphic Design & Production: Héctor Navarro
Layout: Daniel Álvarez
Text: Contribuited by the architects, edited by
Jacobo Krauel and Amber Ockrassa

© Cover photograph: Kim Zwarts

ISBN: 84-89861-68-4
D.L.: B-41479-2003
Impresso na Barcelona, Espanha.

© All languages (except Spanish)
Carles Broto i Comerma
Ausias Marc 20, 4-2
08010 Barcelona, Spain
Tel.: +34 93 301 21 99
Fax: +34-93-302 67 97

minimalist
spaces

index

introduction

Minimalism in architecture is a working method in which the aesthetic seeks all its force and capacity to astonish in a simple way and without superfluous elements. It is said that "less is more", and the spaces are adapted to an idea of life that is intended to be simple, allowing the fascination to be shown in the linearity of a wall, in the smooth textures of a floor, in a reserved space, in the hole as a structuring element of this architecture that seeks its essences. Absence is therefore a virtue that exalts formality, imagination and an appetite for creating new sensations with the minimum intervention. It is the architecture of silence, of subtle expressions that seek the complicity of its occupants and of the context in which it is located. It is for this reason that Minimalism is far more than the simple design of buildings or public spaces, far more than a reduction to simplicity. It also requires a great effort —often even greater than that made by other architectural tendencies— because fewer elements means fewer possibilities and alternatives, and it is

more difficult to achieve amenable, well illuminated rooms that have a welcoming atmosphere. This last aspect is probably the one that has been most criticised, and Minimalist architecture has often been called cold by those who see no more than the material aspects. However, Minimalism is determined to go farther, creating special spaces for a given public, who are fond of this aesthetics of silence and have a certain culture of space. The dialogue between the buildings and the public takes place both in the forms and in spirituality: it is the architecture of calm, reflection and meditation.

The selection of projects presented in this book offers some of the works designed by the best architects in this field at the present time. It concentrates on the works of famous architects such as John Pawson, Shigeru Ban, Tadao Ando and Anouska Hempel, and is excellently illustrated with photographs, plans and construction details that help the reader to understand the work of their creators.

Vincent van Duysen
Finca a Mallorca
Mallorca, Spain

This house maintains the characteristics and spirit of the original Majorcan vernacular architecture on the outside, whilst creating a clean contemporary image on the inside suitable for a holiday home.

The project began with an old country house in the inland part of the island with a theatrical portico of the main facade and two adjacent buildings that function as the custodian's lodging and the owner's office. Van Duysen also worked on the design of the garden, creating visual connections by means of paving in a particular composite of concrete and local stone, also used for the flooring of the buildings to create a sense of indoor-outdoor continuity. An imposing wooden enclosure defines a true barrier, both physical and visual, between the private residential space and the custodian's lodging, or between the world inside and world outside.

As the visitor crosses the threshold he has the impression of entering a large patio, which is nevertheless intimate and welcoming. The only theatrical presence in this space is a washstand made of a single block of stone, inserted in a niche. This sensation continues inside the main house. The entrance area is an empty room, with wood paneling on the walls, concealing the access to the guest bathroom. From the entrance one proceeds to the large kitchen/dining room or to the staircase leading to the upper level housing the bedrooms.

The rigour of the furnishing solutions for each room, based on simple planes and elementary volumes, solids and space, elements for storage and display, seems to make reference to a monastic model of living. The sensory richness of the materials used (sanded and stained oak, stone, marble, ceramics) gives these solutions an air of extreme elegance. Meticulous attention was paid to detail and to the choice of delicate colour combinations to create a relaxing atmosphere for this holiday home.

Photographs: Alberto Piovano

On this double page, views of the kitchen and the dining room. This space, located on the ground floor, is the main room of the dwelling. The kitchen was designed as an open space that is totally integrated in the dining room.

The rooms located on the upper floor give a greater sense of withdrawal and privacy. Much of the furniture used for the different rooms was made with unvarnished wood of very gentle colours.

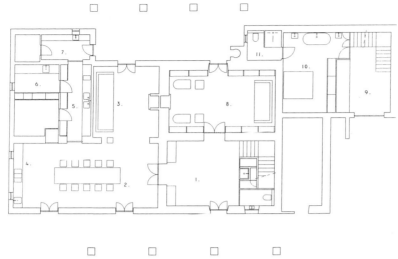

Ground floor plan

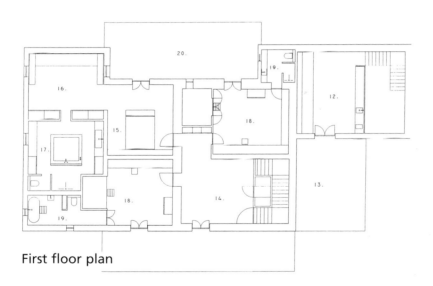

First floor plan

1. Main entrance	11. Shower guesthouse
2. Dining room	12. Kitchen guesthouse
3. Living room	13. Terrace guesthouse
4. Kitchen	14. Nighthall
5. Scullery	15. Master bedroom
6. Laundry	16. Dressing master bedroom
7. Back entrance	17. Master bathroom
8. Library	18. Bedroom child
9. Entrance guesthouse	19. Bathroom child
10. Bedroom & bathroom guesthouse	20. Terrace mainhouse

On the left page, a partial view of the main bathroom. On the right, detailed views of the exquisite washbasin located in the entrance area. This is housed in a natural wooden closet located at the bottom of the staircase leading to the upper floor.

Mark Guard Architects
Refurbishment of a House in Kensal Rise
London, UK

The original building, a car repair shop, consisted of a two-storey brick building with garages covered with pitched roofing on each side. The architect's mission was to create a two-bedroom house in this building. By removing the rudimentary roofing they created and entrance court on one side and a walled garden on the other.

To provide views of Saint Paul's church and Greenwich, bays were opened in the east facade, and the living room and kitchen were placed on the upper floor. The bedrooms on the ground floor open onto the garden. The wall is replaced by sliding window partitions: on the ground floor and on the upper floor, these panels can slide completely to open the space onto the garden. In the studio, glass panels can also disappear in order to eliminate all limits between the inside and the outside. The architects tried to explore the possibilities of a garden on two levels with views to every level in order to relate the living-room with the roof terrace of the studio. Independent concrete walls define the spaces inside the garden and support the steel reinforcement beams of the existing structure and the frames of the sliding bays.

An axis joining the entrance court to the garden through the house is underlined by a strip of water and a new door in the enclosed garden, which is the end of the axis and may also serve as an independent entrance to the studio. A walkway will later join the living-room to the studio terrace. At the top of the staircase a glass bench accentuates the transparency and preserves the visual relationship between the ground floor and the lounge.

The floors are in rough concrete, a subtle reference to the gravel of the garden. The walls are treated as white screens and the narrow kitchen is clad in stainless steel like a ship's kitchen. All interior and exterior doors, and even the shutters, are sliding.

Photographs: John Edward Linden / Arcaid

The site is divided into two different gardens by two walls between which the dwelling is developed. On this double page, views of this interesting space, with the small study built at the opposite end of the dwelling.

To the left, in the foreground, a view of the study. Behind this is the bottom of a narrow staircase leading directly to a small terrace located on the upper level.

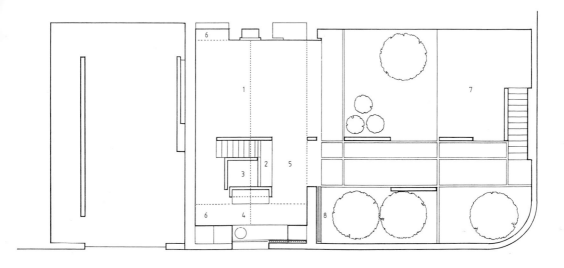

First floor plan

1. Living area
2. Glass bench
3. Void
4. Kitchen
5. Dining-room
6. Roof-light
7. Roof terrace
8. Sliding glass screens

1. Studio
2. Pool
3. Stepping stones
4. Sliding glass screens
5. Garden
6. Guest bedroom
7. Bathroom
8. Master bedroom
9. Shower
10. Entrance courtyard
11. Roof light

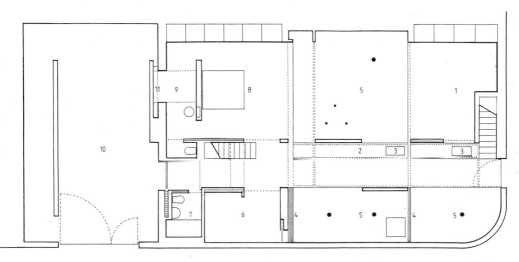

Ground floor plan

Engelen Moore
House in Redfern
Sydney, Australia

This two-storey house has been built on a vacant plock of land formerly occupied by two terrace houses, in a street including houses, warehouses and apartments of varying ages and scales. The local council insisted that it read as two terraced-type houses rather than as a warehouse. The front elevation is divided into two vertical bays. The major horizontal elements are aligned with, and each bay relates proportionally to the adjoining terraced houses. The internal planning reflects this two-bay arrangement at the front, while the rear elevation expresses the full 6 metre high by 7 metre wide internal volume. There was a very limited budget for this project, so a simple strategy was developed to construct a low-cost shell comprised of a steel portal framed structure with concrete block external skins to the long sides, lined with plasterboard internally. The front and rear parapets and blade walls are clad with compressed fibre cement sheets. This shell is painted white throughout. Within this white shell are placed a series of more refined and rigorously detailed elements differentiated by their aluminium or grey paint finish. The front elevation is composed of six vertical panels, the lower level being clad in Alucobond aluminium composite sheet, the left hand panel being the 3.3-metre high front door and the three panels on the right hand side form the garage door. The upper level is made up of operable extruded aluminium louvers, enabling it to adjust from the transparent to the completely opaque.

The six-metre high west-facing glass wall is made up of six individual panels which slide and stack to one side allowing the entire rear elevation to be opened up. This not only spatially extends the interior into the courtyard, but in combination with the louvered front elevation allows exceptional control of cross ventilation to cool the house in summer, while allowing very good solar penetration to warm the house in winter. In summer, this western glass wall is screened from the sun by a large eucalyptus tree on the adjoining property.

Photographs: Ross Honeysett

The main facade is divided into two bays, whereas the rear facade is a single volume 6 metres high by 7 metres wide.

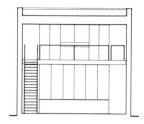

When the six glass panels forming the rear facade are wide open, they extend the interior of the dwelling towards the garden.

Cross section

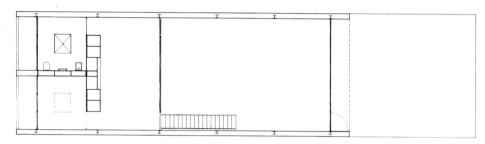

First floor plan

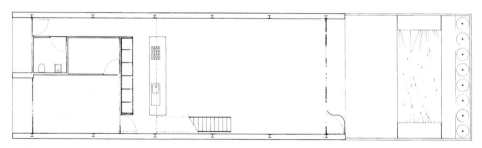

Ground floor plan

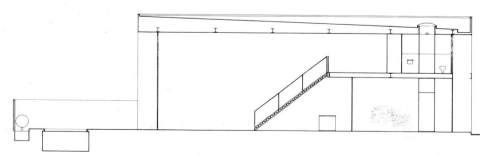

Longitudinal section

The rooms of the upper floor are fitted with mobile aluminium shutters that can be total-ly transparent or totally opaque. The furniture was designed by the architects. The basic premises were low cost and lightness for easy mobility.

Shigeru Ban
2/5 House
West Japan

The 15x25 m rectangular plan of this house is divided into five zones each of 15x5 m. From the south, these zones are: front garden, interior space, central courtyard, interior space, back garden. The house is bounded on its east and west sides by two-store reinforced concrete walls. In order to create the 2/5 (i.e. 2 by 1/5) first floor space, enclosed glass boxes, similar to that of the Mies van de Rohe's Farnsworth House, were positioned across the second floor. The spaces created beneath these have a Japanese sensibility in which interior and exterior are linked both visually and physically. This contrasts with the merely visual spatial connectivity of Mies' work. The first floor is a "universal floor": a unified space within which each of the functional elements is placed, while at the same time the use of sliding doors at the boundary between interior and exterior, and the manually operated tent roof results in a sense both of enclosure and openness. The screen on the road side is formed from bent, punched aluminium which folds up accordion-like to form the garage door. On the north side, a grid of PVC gutters have been hung as planters, creating a dense screen which ensures privacy.

Photographs: Hiroyuki Hirai

The facade of the dwelling that gives onto the street is clad with a sheet of perforated corrugated metal that offers a high degree of privacy and creates a special visual connection with the exterior.

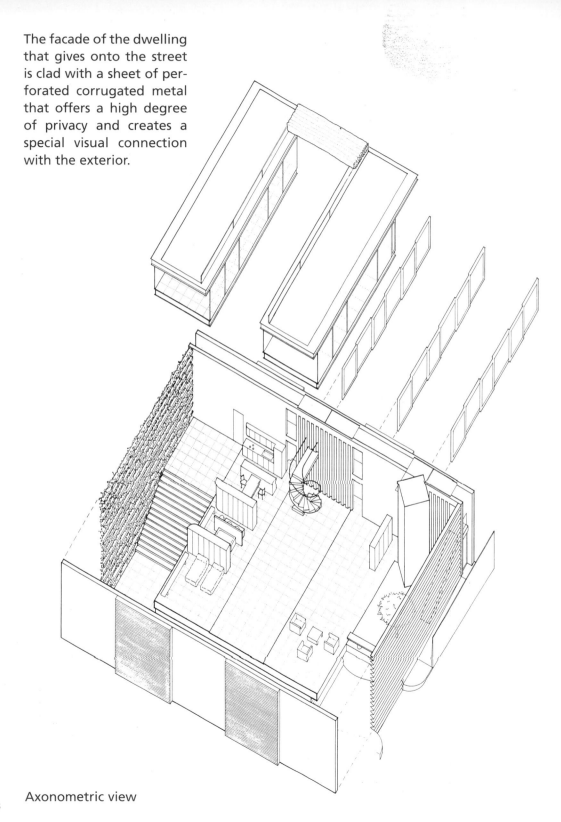

Axonometric view

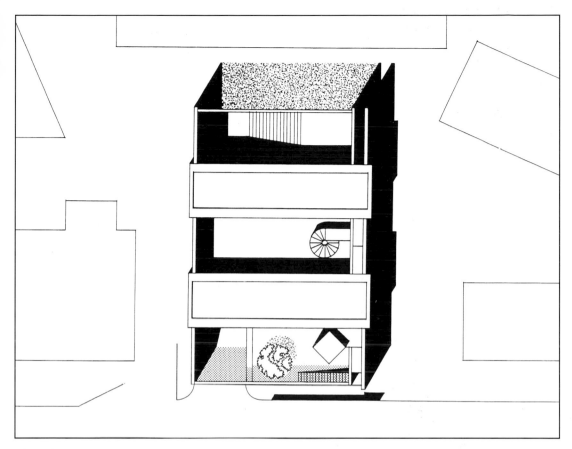

Site plan

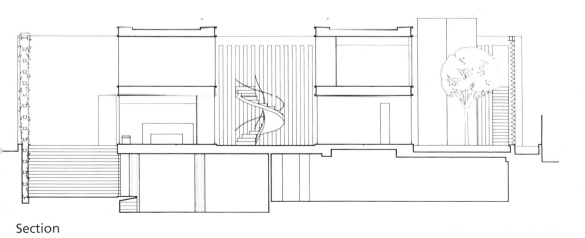

Section

The spaces of the dwelling are impregnated with a Japanese sensibility, whose maximum expression is found in the delicate presence of the surrounding nature (the front and rear gardens) in the interior of the dwelling.

Vincent van Duysen
Town Houses in Flandres
Flandres, Belgium

The project consists in the refurbishment of a classic 30's row house with a fairly restricted width and a deep plan.

The house is situated between five similar row houses by the same architect and from the same period; which is why the front elevation has only been restored and is further kept untouched.

The deep plan of the existing house made it very dark what Van Duysen has completely abolished in favour of an open plan with a glazed central void over three stories visually connecting all the spaces vertically and horizontally, daylight pouring an extensive rooflight and a completely glazed back elevation.

The impressive spatial qualities are emphasized by several factors. From one side, the unrestricted views, got from the front to the back of the house on all levels (entering through the front door one can see the garden gate in the back garden). Those views come as well from two voids on the rooflight and the central lightwell; the completely glazed back elevation give views of the old industrial buildings and chimneys.

The materials used in the building process consists of flush planes of dark tinted oak against a background of white plastered walls and is carefully proportioned to emphasize the spatial system of the house. Large planes of glass divide the structure and organization of the plan.

The whole building is opened up to the garden through the completely glazed elevation, whereby the window frames again reflect the structure inside. At the same time, the walled garden elongates the space of the dining and cooking area and combined with the void above the dining room and the use of identical stone floor in and outside, effectively pulls the internal and external space together in one. The patio wall marks the end of the external dining area and creates a kind of "garden room", with a framed view onto the rest of the planted garden.

Photographs: Jan Verlinde

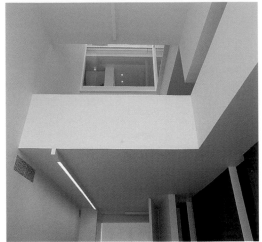

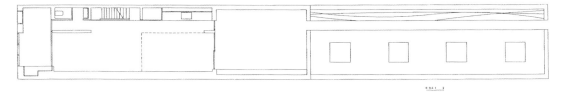

Ground floor plan

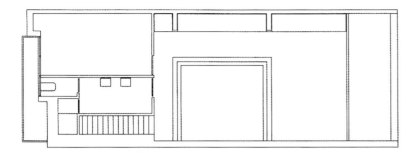

Third floor plan

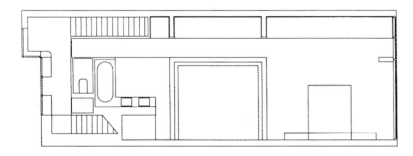

Second floor plan

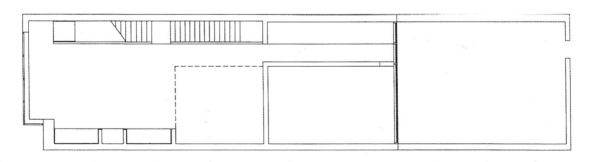

First floor plan

Cross section

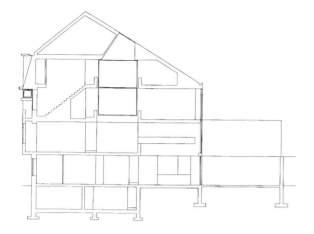

The material used by Van Duysen in the building process of this house consist of flush planes of dark tinted oak which constrat against an inmaculate background of white plastred walls.

John Pawson
Maison Pawson
London, UK

The project is based in the restoration of a dwelling in a Victorian terraced house in London. The facade of the building remains unaltered except for the recession of the new entrance door leading to the raised ground floor where the two original reception rooms are transformed into one space retaining both working fireplaces.

A stone bench on the long wall acts as seating, hearth and light source. The interior atmosphere is minimal and comfortable. A table with benches and two loose chairs are only furniture. On the opposite wall a row of pivoting doors conceal storage.

Opaque white blinds screen the windows. Douglas fir boards are laid uncut from the front of the building to the back, extending as far as the garden balcony.

A new set of straight stairs leads to the bathroom. The bath, the floor, basin cube, and bench running around the edge of the room -which also contains the lavatory- are all made from the same cream coloured stone. Gaps in the floor drain water from the shower mounted directly on the wall, and brimming over the edge of the bath. This is and attempt to capture some of the qualities with which bathing was once approached, more as a ritual than hurried functional necessity.

On the same floor the two children's rooms have beds, shelves and desks in the same wood with pinboard forming one complete wall. The top floor, suffused with natural light, is devoted to the main bedroom. In the simple gallery kitchen, storage for food cutlery and crockery is on one side, while the appliances are on the other.

Materials are used as simply and directly as possible. The two white Carrara marble worktops are not surfaces, but elements in their own right, four inches thick and over fourteen feet long. Holes have been cut for the marble sink and the iron cooking range.

The kitchen's balcony gives access down to the garden which is laid out as another room with stone floor, table and bench and a high trellis on the tree sides.

Photographs: Richard Glover

With the exception of those that look onto the rear courtyard, the windows are made of etched glass. The kitchen was equipped with two large working areas made in Carrara marble.

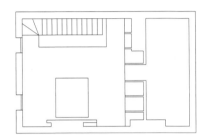

First floor plan

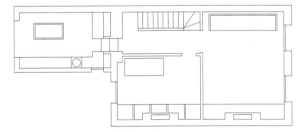

Ground floor plan

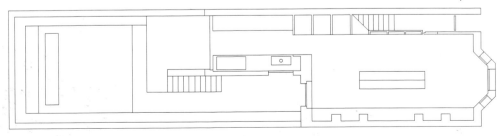

Cross section

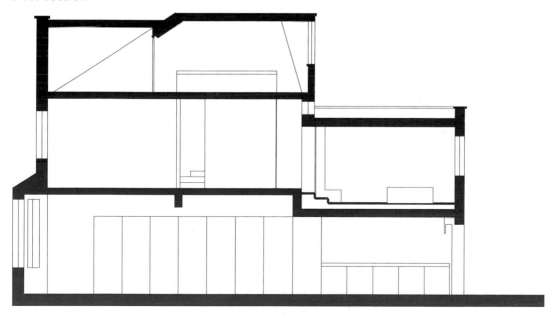

In the bathroom, both the bathtub and the washbasin were made in stone of a soft cream colour. The floor and walls are clad in the same material.

Tadao Ando
Lee House
Tokyo, Japan

This private house is situated on a hill in suburbs not far from the Tokyo metropolitan centre, Funabashi, and occupies a site area of 484 sq m. The location of the site at an intersection and its comfortable size (in comparison with more normal dimensions in Japanese houses) have allowed the creation of numerous additional spaces to the house: courts, gardens and terraces.

Small garden courts of varying character are stacked on different levels within the house in order to grant each court a distinct realms and infuse variation into the house space.

Overall, the house has a three-level rectangular core with a 5x21 m plant. An internal atrium is positioned in the mid-section of this rectangular structure, with rooms positioned on either end. The rooms face each other across the atrium at staggered half-floor intervals, and are connected by ramps running parallel to the court.

The ground floor houses the living-room and dining-room where the family gathers, while individual bedrooms are arranged on the upper floors. The gentle, green slope of the garden draws close where it is viewed from the dining room. This garden invites nature into the lives of the residents, while maintaining the house's privacy by obstructing visibility from outside. The different garden courts ensure a dwelling space that offers its occupants continual rediscovery, within daily life, of their relationship with the city and nature.

Photographs: Mitsuo Matsuoka

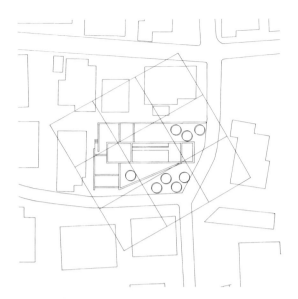

Stepped levels, courts and terraces add complexity to the project which is nevertheless regulated by a web system.

Site plan

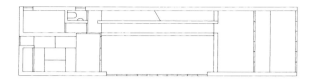

First floor plan

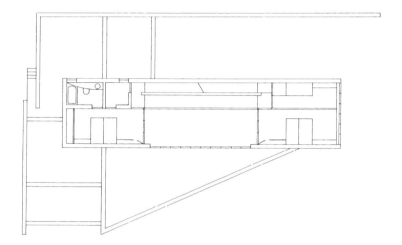

Ground floor plan

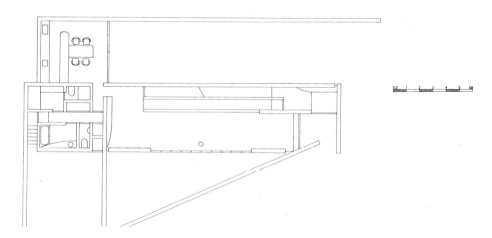

Basement plan

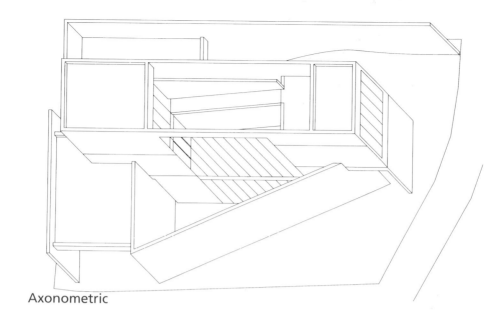

Axonometric

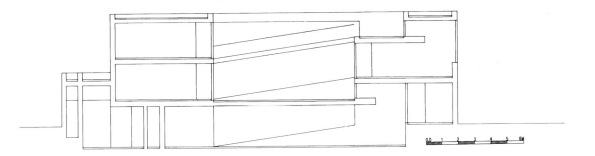

Section

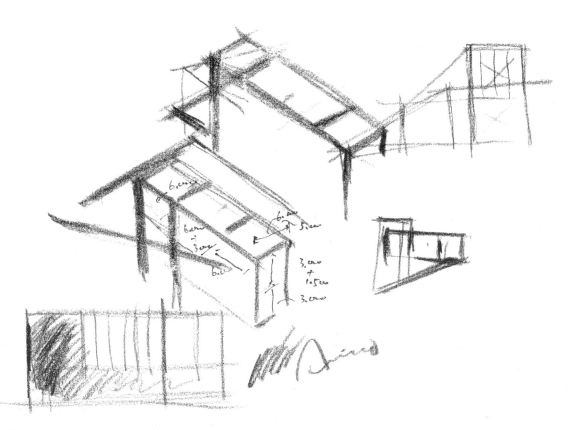

The dramatic contrast between high concrete walls, the intensity of the light provided by large openings and the subtle yet notable presence of nature are to be contemplated. Tadao Ando skilfully combines the complexity of the spaces with the simplicity of the house's rectangular base.

Graham Phillips
Skywood House
Middlessex, UK

The home's plot, etched into a densely populated zone, was subject to zoning laws which restricted the surface area available for construction to 250 sq m. The architect set out to create a "glass box" in the forest, a structure whose boundaries between interior and exterior would be blurred, where water would play a leading role.

The house, lying before the shores of a lake, is reached via a black gravel walkway which winds around the house, ending at the main patio at the back. The building rests on a grey limestone plinth, its bare, unadorned surface highlighting its simple shapes. Frameless glass doors covered by a pergola, a design echoed in the entrance to the garage, from the main entryway. A noteworthy element in the exterior space is the main chimney, which hides the drainage system, the pipes and the ventilation system within a single unit. The dwelling is unified by long, 3-metre-high walls which reach beyond the enclosed spaces toward the lake and surrounding terrain, thereby defining footpaths. This minimalist expression contrasts with the wealth of the landscape, creating a serene, yet wondrous, experience.

The dwelling is enclosed by two glass wings, the first of which, at a height of 3 metres, forms the volume containing the four bedrooms and their respective bathrooms. This module comprises one of the sides of a completely enclosed garden, which has a square lawn lying over a border of black gravel.

The glass volume which houses the sitting room is the tallest, thereby highlighting the steel sheet which comprises the floating roof. The main space enjoys breathtaking views across the lake to the west, toward the island, as much a focal point by night as by day.

The tiling of the sitting room continues outward toward the garden, through a glass facade, blurring the boundaries between interior and exterior. This space is organised like a double square: the sitting room is defined by a 3.6 sq m carpet centred over limestone flooring, a motif —that of a square framed within another background— which is seen again in the inside patio and the garden at the back. In the kitchen/dining room, a combination of sliding panels and two moveable tables allow a distribution which can be altered according to its user's needs.

Photographs: Nigel Young

The artificial lake, a huge pond with geotextile protection layers under a foot of soil, is supplied by an 80-metre-foot deep well and is sharply framed by the lawn. Reflections from the water create a constantly changing array of light inside the dwelling.

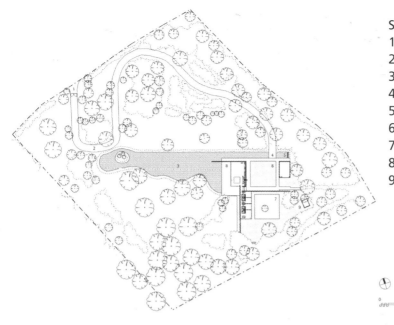

Site plan
1.Entry
2.Drive
3.Lake
4.Bridge
5.Waterwall
6.Courtyard
7.Walled Garden
8.Terrace
9.Logstore

0   30m

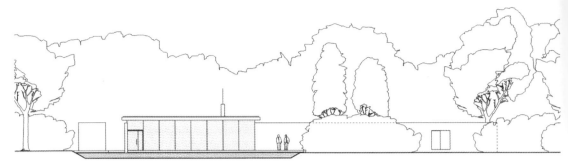

West elevation

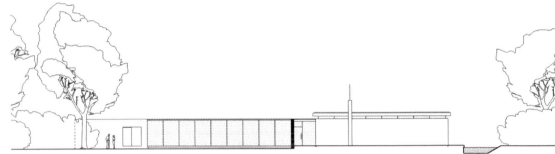

East elevation

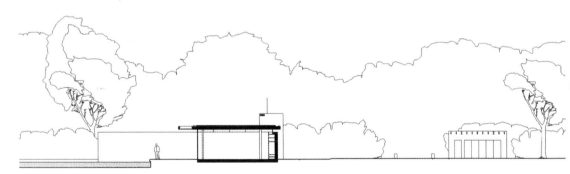

East-west section through lake, living-room and courtyard

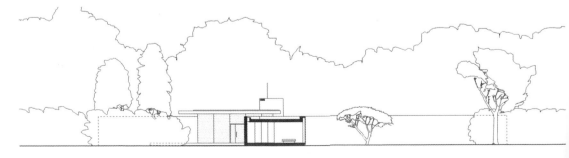

East-west section through master bedroom and garden

Limestone and glass, used both inside and out, confer homogeneity on the building and continuity between the exterior and interior.

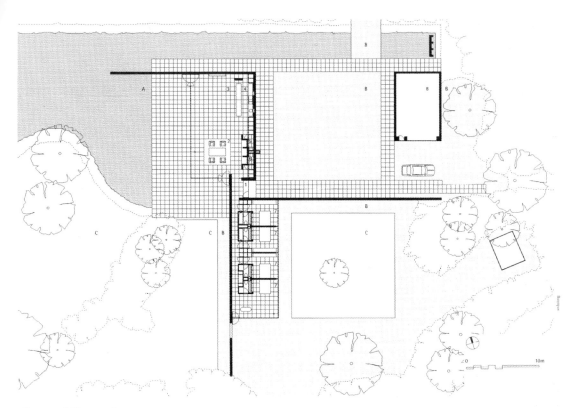

Ground floor plan

The entirety of the water, electrical and ventilation systems are operated through a single vertical duct, while the heating system is underground, thereby avoiding the need for radiators. The furniture and other decorative elements have been custom-designed for this home.

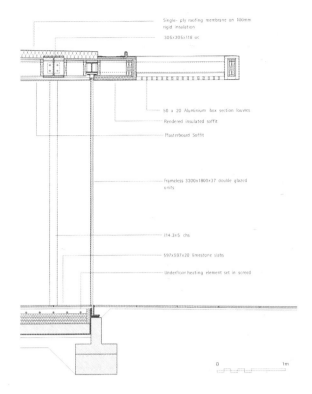

Single- ply roofing membrane on 100mm rigid insulation

305x305x118 uc

50 x 20 Aluminium box section louvres

Rendered insulated soffit

Plasterboard Soffit

Frameless 3300x1800x37 double glazed units

114.3x5 chs

597x597x20 limestone slabs

Underfloor heating element set in screed

0   1m

Section detail

Adolf H. Kelz & Hubert Soran
Mittermayer's House
Salzburg, Austria

In the conversion of this two-century-old house near Salzburg the architects have used a combination of two approaches. The original building was divided into two main parts: the original stone building and a wooden shed. The stone building has been conserved with its internal distribution, but the shed has been converted into a big glass box with wooden joinery, within which the rooms hang from the hipped roof.

The glazed box which occupies approximately half of the main building forms the most radical aspect of this scheme. The structural elements of steel and wood are separated from the glazed skin. The living/dining area on the ground floor has an open plan and is overlooked by galleries, while the rooms are white plywood boxes suspended in the space created within the glass box. All the spaces are independent units integrated into a whole and conjugated by spiral staircases, galleries and walkways that create exciting perspectives. The program includes four bedrooms for the owner's children, a library and a restroom.

The roof has been conserved almost intact, only interrupted by a strip window and a skylight for the loft. It tempers the contrast between old and new and brings unity to the whole. A small refurbished annex with a new zinc roof contains the garage, sauna and some utilities.

Photographs: Angelo Kaunat

The conventional circulation systems have been replaced by walkways, galleries and spiral staircases that communicate the different spaces. Views of the ground floor living area. The wood and steel structural elements do not touch the facade of the building.

Pascal van der Kelen
Haemelinck-Van der Kelen House
Stekene, Belgium

This house, which is the architect's own dwelling, is a manifesto of the synthetic and essential language that is distilled in all the works of Van der Kelen. The volume rises on a small and narrow site, which led the architect to design a long volume, contained and silent, with white walls and large glazed openings that run along one of its long sides, establishing a permanent dialogue between the concise garden, the surrounding trees and the interior of the dwelling.

The construction is conceived as a white box of 10x20 metres whose measurements are strictly proportional to the other elements of the project —the garden, the orchard, the garage volume, the warehouse and facilities, the space of the roads and the terraces.

A single loadbearing wall of 15 metres crosses the dwelling from the hall of the north entrance to the south end where the living area is located. A contrast there arises between the vertical nature of the hall, developed in the space framed by the two walls, and the horizontal nature of the living room with the views toward the landscape through a 6 metre wide opening and a 15 metre window that looks onto the orchard.

On the exterior, another wall 35 metres long separates the path from the courtyard located on the west side of the house. A second wall works as a screen from the exterior and leads the visitors from the garden to the entrance located on the north side of the house. The architect has hardly intervened in the old garden, only adding a few new trees and rectangular flower beds.

One of the most outstanding features of the project can be seen in the accesses and the circulation. A procession-like path runs along the whole length of the building and connects the street to the garden at the north entrance of the house. This path also traces an "architectural promenade" in the interior through the most public spaces of the dwelling and culminates in the intimacy of the bedrooms. The single floor is divided into two parts: the environment that houses the living-room, the dining room and the kitchen, contained on the west side, and —separated from these areas by a wall— the bedrooms, toilets and work area, all of which are housed at the east end.

In the whole interior one notes the spatial continuity that is created through fragmentation of the dividing elements. Low walls function as screens and create open sequences with a flowing interrelation of rooms. The chromatic homogeneity of the whole dwelling and the minimum language of the furniture that dominates the decor also intensify this aspect.

Photographs: Alberto Piovano

Thanks to the great transparency of the facades, the exterior landscape is constantly perceived from the interior of the dwelling.

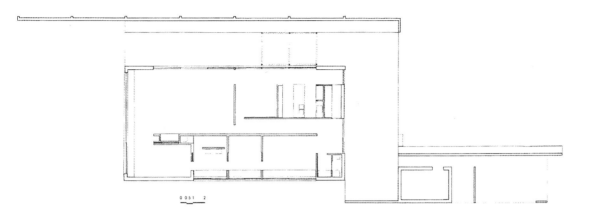

Kei'ichi Irie
T House
Tokyo, Japan

This house was built in a residential area in central Tokyo. Two separate households live on the first floor, and a family with four members resides on the second and third floors. The introduction of multi-dimensional analysis into the architectural structure has instantly expanded the possibilities of overall views. Many features of this T house are indebted to structural engineer's work in structure design: possibilities of arranging a huge top-light or thin pillars without any restriction; floor hollowed out in cylindrical shape; and beamless slabs. Here, state-of-the-art technology is probably at its best, attributing an unpretentious, nonchalant view onto the output.

The overall composition, based on a simple arrangement of a circle and a square, consists of three elements: floors carved out by freely positioned skylights and cylinders, 15 slender columns (250 mm), and a flat slab (250 mm). The structure was determined through multi-dimensional analysis. Composed of rectangles and the circles of the cylinders, the second and third floors are partitioned by large sliding doors, but are fundamentally horizontally and vertically continous; the overall space is apprehended as one fluidly connected space. Inside the space there is a cylinder (bathroom) and a cube (sanity room). The first floor is treated as a base, partly composed of piloti, and is painted in monochrome (yellow), unlike the upper floors.

Photographs: Hiroyuki Hirai

Basement floor plan

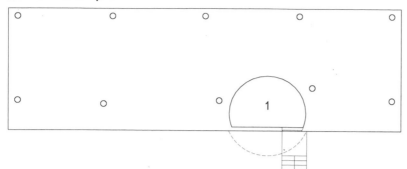

Ground floor plan

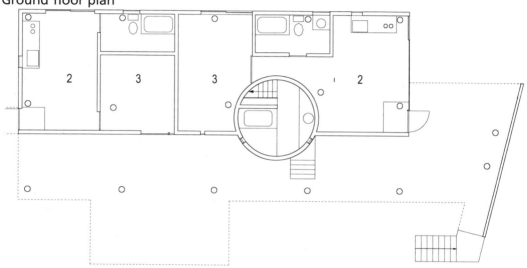

First floor plan

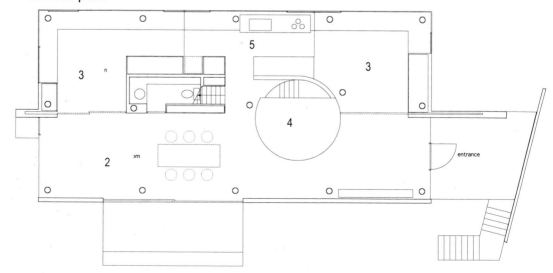

entrance

Second floor plan

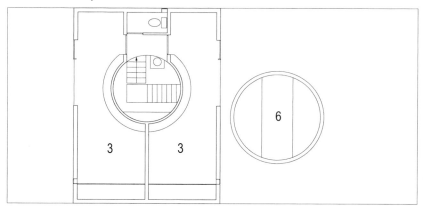

The spaces of the dwelling are defined by geometric and chromatic elements. The use of three basic colours —black, red and white— and the predominance of elementary forms —the square and the circle— organise the distribution of the space and create different atmospheres inside the building.

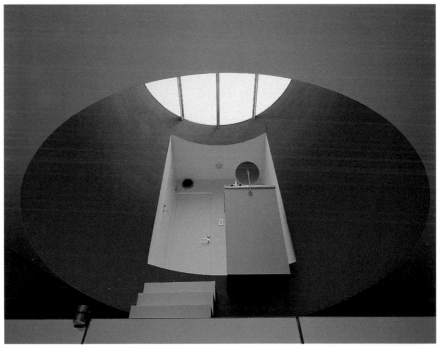

Anouska Hempel
The Hempel
London, UK

Discreetly hidden just north of Hyde Park, the Hempel Hotel and Hempel Garden Square are a unique phenomenon in London.

The simplicity and silence of the Orient and their metamorphism into the Western world, with the most innovative global technology, create a very special hotel. A row of perfectly restored white Georgian houses and a private garden surrounded by trees give little hint of the remarkable transformation within.

Crossing the main entrance is almost a mystical experience. Beyond it, the visitor finds a wide empty space, in which the only outstanding element is the monolithic block of the reception desk, which recalls the calm and contemplative atmosphere of a temple. In this same area, a lighted fireplace under an atrium through which natural light penetrates gently invites the guests to take a seat as a ritual performance rather than a banal action. In the remaining rooms, the same simple and exquisite architecture models spaces bathed in warm indirect lighting, rooms perfumed with oriental essences, beds that are an invitation to deep repose, a washbasin with an illuminated heart

The visitor will be immediately struck by the openness and the simplicity of the materials and colours: beige Portland stone for the floors, black Belgian stone and granite in the bathrooms, golden chalk and sand colours for the lower floors, rust, grey or black for the upper floors.

All rooms have been individually designed to offer the discerning traveler an alternative, a modern definition of luxury: telephones, fax line, modem facility, air-conditioning, CD and video player, oxygen in the mini-bars. There are four function rooms, private dining rooms, video conferencing facilities, libraries, fitness room, private apartments and even the temporary illusion of a tent in the Zen garden square or cocktails served on the terrace to 150 people.

For Anouska Hempel, the hotel's creator the Hempel is consequence of the desire for radical change. The result is a very special place that revolutionizes the concepts of travelling and accommodation in the threshold of a new century.

Photographs: Kim Zwarts

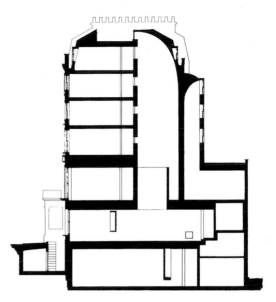

The photographs on this page show the reception area and the large five-storey atrium through which natural light penetrates in the lobby and the corridor in front of the rooms.

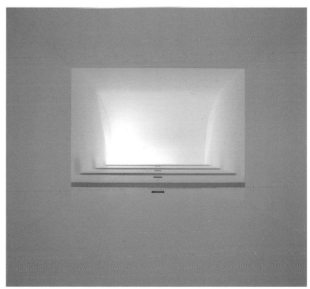

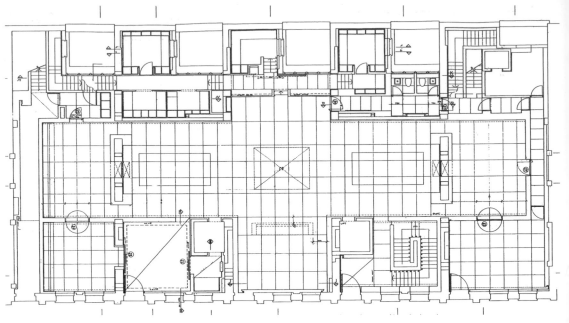

Ground floor plan

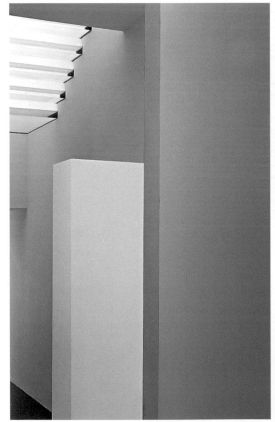

All the rooms have been designed independently. Nevertheless, in all of them a common interior design creates simple and exquisite spaces where light plays a leading role.

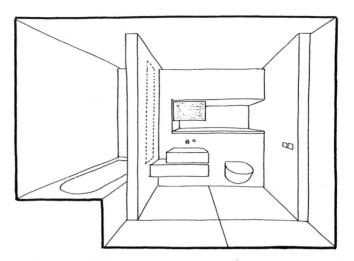

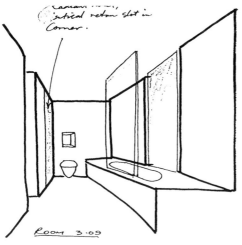

Vertical return slot in Corner.

ROOM 3.09

Claudio Lazzarini & Carl Pickering
Nil Bar
Rome, Italy

Located on the basement floor of a former bakery in an upmarket residential area of Rome, near famous Villa Borghese, the Nil bar-restaurant was a challenge to the architects Lazzarini and Pickering in collaboration with Giuseppe Postet and Fabio Sonnino. The bar was done on a tight schedule: three months during the summer of 1997. The space to remodel —a long basement corridor— was unprepossessing. The architects hollowed it out to make a soundproof shell. The project's main idea was simple:"a blank page on which to write, spatially and graphically".

The space is laid out around three dramatized architectural elements: a runway that becomes a continuous bench which serves as a podium as well, a system of white curtains that open and close spaces and perspectives, a bar-pole, which is both a screen and a volume of light. The long, slighty elevated footway in bleached maple works like a stage: people walking on it can see and can be seen. After dinner it doubles as a bench or even a dance floor.

The Nil was designed to be constantly changing. Everything is movement and reflexion, technological imagery and magnetic waves. Electric curtains alter perspectives; digitally regulated halogen lighting, with its variations, seems to scan the beat of the place; a video-projector system floods the interior with moving colours. Beneath its apparent unity, the layout plays on subtle constrasts: on a monochrome field styles, materials and periods blend in a typically Italian salute to the sixties. The space can be become pink or blue; optical or polka dot, water; fire or forest or be covered in images of magnetic waves, television interferences, images from the biological world, etc. The space is also a screen for video art: works by artists Paolo Canevari and Adrian Tranquilli have been projected.

The large pieces of roman travertine become places on which to sit, sing or dance. On the other hand, the logo of Nil is a white bar code printed on acetate that represents the curtains, central element of the project. The stark whiteness of Nil is not its most interesting element, but rather its changeability of image, space and music (a recurring theme in the designer's work).

Photographs: Matteo Piazza

As can be seen in the succession of images on the right, a system of white electric curtains opens and closes the spaces and the visual perspectives. In the foreground, large elements of Roman travertine in places that can be used for seating, looking or dancing on it.

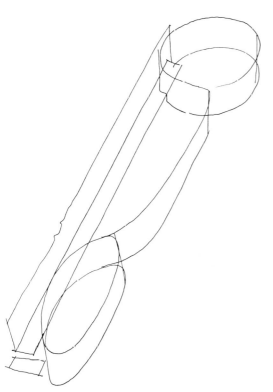

Diagram of the curtain system

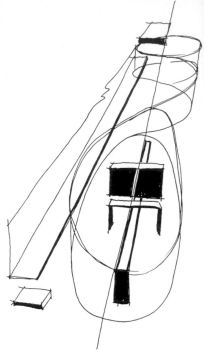

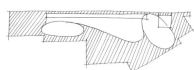

Conceptual sketch

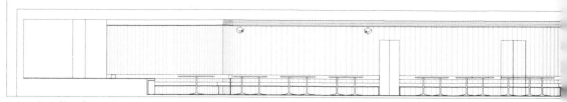

Longitudinal section

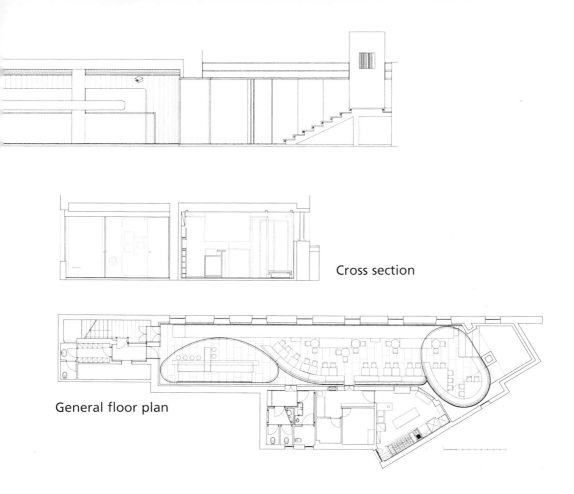

Cross section

General floor plan

The combination of mobile curtains and the image projection system provides infinite spatial possibilities. The project benefits from a magical interplay of form, light and colour, causing a sensation of absolute theatricality and variation.

Ronald Hoolf
New Deli
Amsterdam, The Netherlands

Located in the centre of Amsterdam, this is a small colourful and essential restaurant with a powerful graphic content. The first thing that strikes the eye is the chromatic quality of the red-painted walls combined with the delicate and elegant shades of beige, brown and white of the rest of the establishment, which gives this space an unmistakable image.

A large clock receives the visitor as an emblem of the permanent opening of the kitchen, which serves exotic dishes twenty-four hours a day.

According to Ronald Hooft, who designed the project with his friend Jen Alkema of Alkema Architects, the aim was to develop a concept of interior design with a highly eclectic approach in order to reflect the type of cuisine and the flexible opening hours.

The project also responds to the need of the owners, Jacob Admiraal and Sander Louwerens, to give New Deli a characteristic and easily repeatable image, because it is intended as the pilot project of a franchising chain.

As a reflection of the high level of creativity and skill that is applied in the kitchen of the New Deli, in which ingredients of several European cultures are used (mostly Mediterranean and East European), elements of a wide variety of styles, countries and periods are incorporated in the design, without losing the balance or running the risk of incorporating an excessively postmodern concept of language. In spite of the Spartan appearance (all the furniture is composed of naked and minimal pieces without upholstery or added elements) great care has been taken to create a comfortable atmosphere. On a more pragmatic and visible level, Hooft, who has an art background and graduated from the Rietveld Academia of Amsterdam, says that he sought inspiration from very diverse sources: from Chinese philosophy to Retro-Futurism, from the graphic design of music videos to the film productions of Hollywood. In combination with several fixed elements, such as the tables and the wall seating, the free-standing furniture features some classic design such as the seats by Arne Jacobsen and the light fittings by Vico Magistretti, which give the premises a serene image of extreme elegance.

Photographs: Mirjam Bleeker

NEWDELI

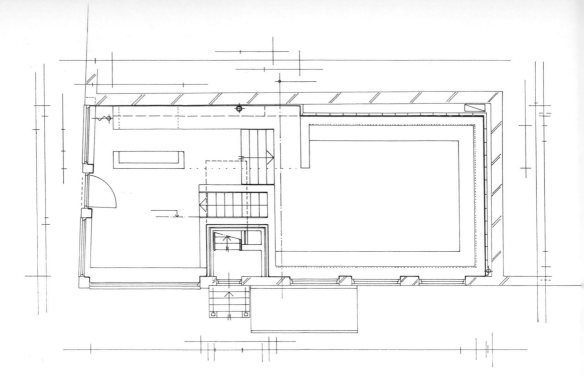

Ground floor plan

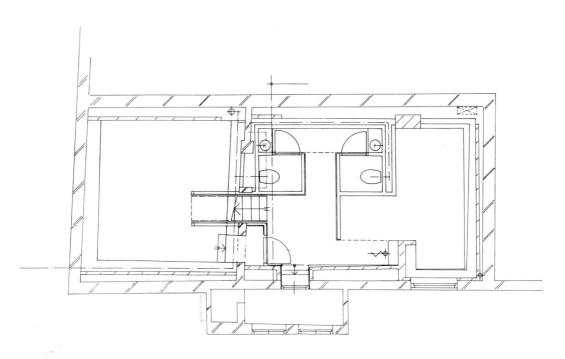

Basement plan

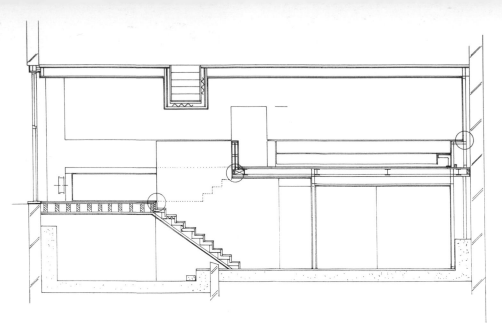

Longitudinal section

The restaurant becomes a contemporary and yet timeless expression of the concept by means of a careful combination of simplicity, light and a strong contrast of colours.

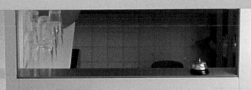

LUNCH ALL DAY

KEUKEN >

NEWDELI

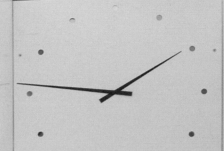

LUNCH ALL DAY

‹ TOILET

KEUKEN ›

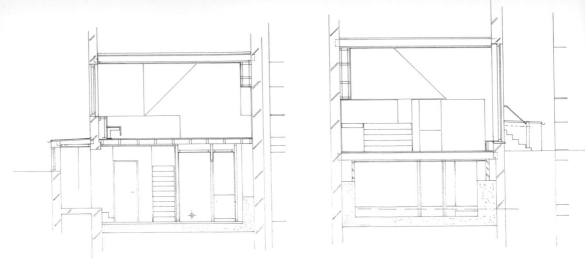

Cross sections

NEWDELI

Claesson Koivisto Rune
Architect's Office
Stockholm, Sweden

For their own office, Claesson Koivisto Rune sought a shop-space in a side street in central Stockholm. They thought that being in contact with the street and the ongoing life of the city was essential for their inspiration and for their availability to clients The architects divided the long and narrow space according to hierarchy. The front room, which opens to the street through a display window and a glass door, became the meeting room. Between this room and the next, two large double-etched glass sheet walls were placed. They let natural light in, and one can pass between them on either side, but they obstruct the vision into the next room. From outside one can sense the continuing space, but not what it contains and not how much there is. Part of the floor is made of glass, illuminating the room beneath. Behind the two glass sheets fluorescent lighting was installed. The tubes are UV-coloured and turned on at night as a light effect.

The next room became the hub of the office: computers, faxes, telephones, etc. This space also houses the lavatory, the kitchen with a small dining area and the stairs down to the lower floor. Downstairs are the library, drawing boards and storage rooms. Finally, under the front room is the model workshop. The background to the design had to be neutral, and thus white was the colour chosen for all the office and the furniture.

In the office there are no doors (except for the storage rooms and lavatory), but the division into rooms/functions is clear. The arrangement of the different spaces allows the architects to choose how far into the design process they let their clients, maybe just the presentation room, maybe all the way into the model production in the workshop. The room hierarchy is also one of order. Design is a messy business, especially model making.

Photographs: Patrick Engquist

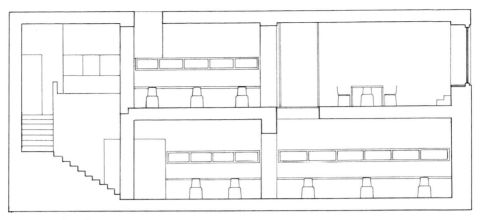

Longitudinal section

The studio is accessed directly from the street. Because the premises were formerly used as a shop, the reception, like a shop window, connects the interior and the exterior. The window and the glass door provide natural light to a semi-basement.

At night, the fluorescent tubes behind the translucent glass panels that separate the reception from the interior of the study reinforce the image of the outer room as a shop window. Behind the panels is the "nucleus" of the study, the production area.

Ground floor plan

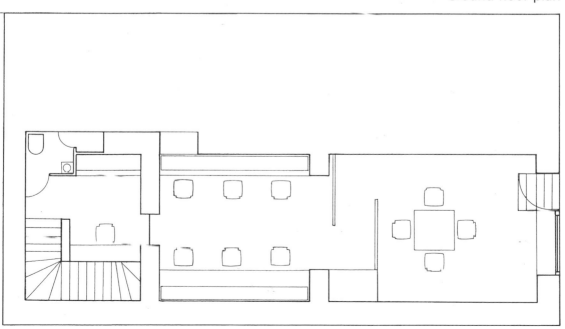

The space is defined by geometric forms and the absolute predominance of white. The audacious use of lighting as a decorative element reinforces the design concept of the scheme.

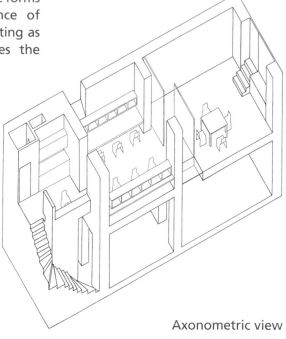

Axonometric view

Studio Archea
House in Costa San Giorgo
Florence, Italy

This apartment designed by Studio Archea is located in an old medieval tower near Ponte Vecchio, in the heart of Florence. The original Renaissance building had large wooden beams that gave it a certain majesty, and the challenge consisted in designing a residential space that took advantage of the exceptional characteristics of the Quattrocento to create a functional and contemporary atmosphere.

The space is designed around a curvilinear stone wall that organises the diverse functions of the dwelling and supports the metal beams of the mezzanine, which is used as the night area. This wall acts as a bookcase, leaves the kitchen semi-concealed, houses in its perimeter the stairwell, and divides the spaces so that the materials define and organise the different atmospheres of the dwelling. An iron staircase set against the opposite wall leads to a platform giving access to the mezzanine. From this horizontal platform, a walkway also leads to a small panoramic pool over the dining room with a bathroom next to it. This area of the upper floor is in the new stone part of the apartment; the rectilinear mezzanine is separated by a small wooden floor space.

Because of the small size of the scheme, the architects were able to design all the elements in detail, avoiding prefabrication and creating unique, almost sculptural objects.

The architects showed great respect for tradition in the use of natural stone, in the conservation of the original ceiling and in the distribution of the furniture. A single space and different atmospheres for one person: this is the result of this intervention in an apartment set between walls full of history.

Photographs: Alessandro Ciampi

The void created between the two main volumes is used as a corridor on the ground floor. On the upper floor, this free space offers different views and perspectives, and opens up the dimensions of the apartment.

Agustí Costa
Dúplex en Navàs
Barcelona, Spain

The peculiar configuration of this 427 sq m maisonette is the result of the action carried out in the interior of the top two floors of a terraced building that was near to completion. The seventh floor already had the outer walls. Some of the layout had also already been established, and it was decided to conserve it as a basis for meeting the requirements of the project. On the eighth floor the architects enjoyed total freedom of action to adapt it to a leisure use, with a covered and heated swimming pool, a sauna, a dressing room, a living-room, a living/dining room, a small kitchen, terraces and a barbecue.

One of the basic principles of the intervention focused on fostering the interaction between the different spaces of the seventh floor through sliding panels, glass and transparencies. The common staircase was also transformed into a private staircase for the maisonette, with differentiated spaces for access on foot and access using the lift to the interior of the dwelling, and with a stairwell that is completely glazed at the top. Another important feature was the conversion of the central ventilation well into a cloister-like, totally glazed volume whose presence extends to the whole dwelling. The capacity for transformation of the spaces on the eighth floor through vertical and horizontal separations allows the exterior to be perceived and felt according to the demands of the moment, and helps to enhance the natural lighting, creating a sensation that one is living outdoors.

Through the treatment of the materials, the two floors were perfectly differentiated, though at the same time the whole dwelling was given a unitary sense. For example, the polished stainless steel is found both in the sliding doors and windows and in the roof structure, the bathrooms and the terrace. Finally, the application of bright colours in the major features determined the character of the rooms. Thus, the lemon yellow on the concrete roof slab of the leisure floor offers brightness, whereas the red on the drop ceiling that runs around the glazed central space on the seventh floor emphasies the singularity of the space, and the blue applied to the wall of the kitchen and the utility room unifies the two spaces, which are separated by a subtle sliding panel of steel and glass, partly acid etched and partly transparent.

Photographs: Eloi Bonjoch / David Cardelús

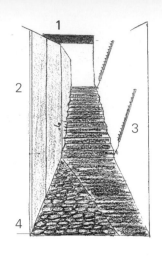

1. Drop ceiling
2. Aluminiun-silver coloured armoured screen
3. Aluminiun-silver strap light
4. Rubber-carpet with luminous shaping

Staircase access to first floor

Section L-2

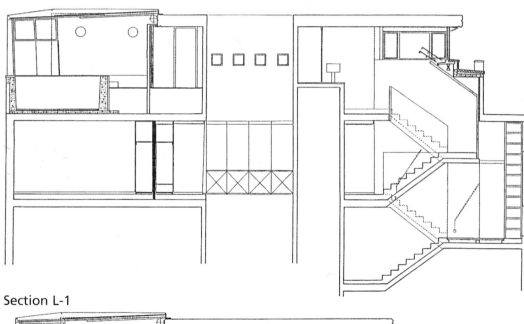

Section L-1

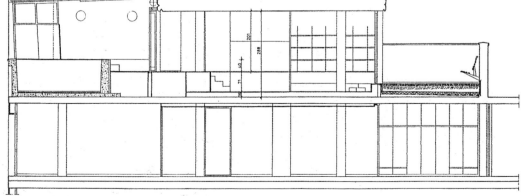

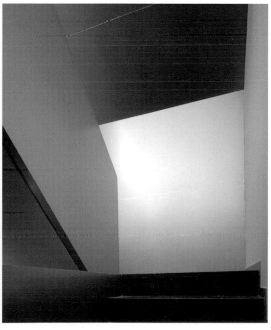

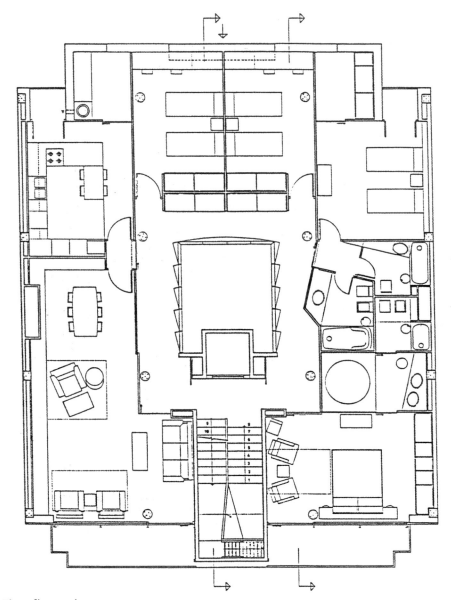

First floor plan

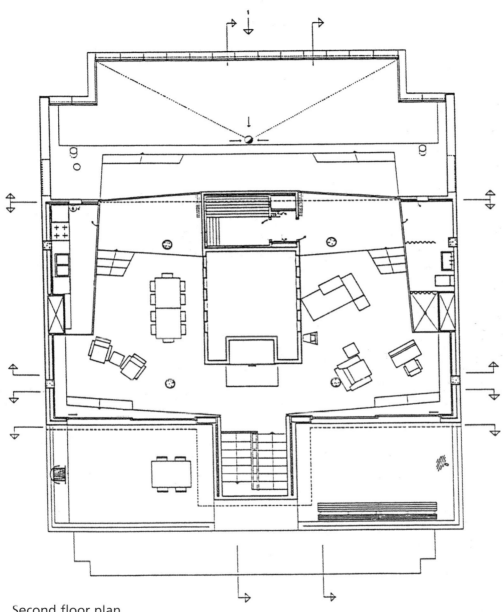

Second floor plan

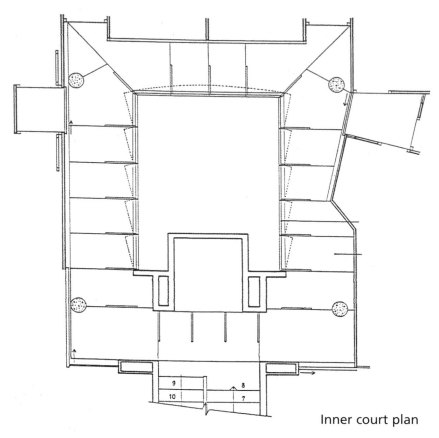

Inner court plan

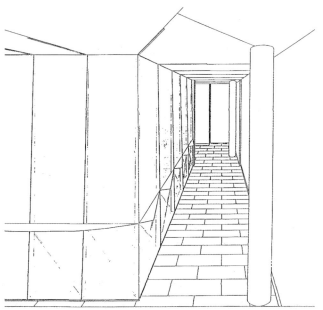

Perspective inner court plan

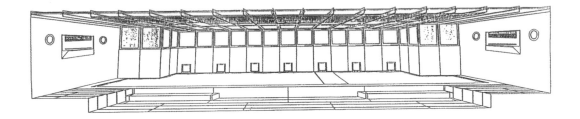

Perspective terrace-swimming pool

John Pawson
Audi apartment
Amsterdam, The Netherlands

The architect John Pawson is the author of this calm and minimal dwelling inside an eighteenth-century building beside a canal in the city of Amsterdam.

As is habitual in this British architect's work, his attitude to the old spaces of this dwelling-studio was silent and moderate, careful and essential. The client, Pierre Audi, the director of the Amsterdam Opera, already knew the architect. In fact, years before, he had commissioned him to design his dwelling in London, when he was working as a theatre director in the city.

For his Dutch apartment, Audi asked Pawson for a fluid and coherent interior with the architectural quality of the historical building, and an interior programme endowed with a certain spatial order.

The functional layout of the building, on six levels, is structured as follows: dining room and kitchen in the basement, study-library on the ground floor and living area, the guest bedrooms with their respective toilets and the main bedroom distributed on the first, second, third and fourth floors. The basement is the level on which Pawson found the largest number of original elements to conserve in his design.

A large original chimney presides over the dining room area, and the kitchen —intercommunicated with the dining room— features the old exhaust hood and the original tiles on the walls.

The access level is a more "public" area, in which a large study area and a small library are developed. On the top floor, the main bedroom is one of the most outstanding spaces. It is characteristic of the buildings in this area of the city, featuring the large exposed wooden beams of the pitched roof.

Photographs: Christopher Kircherer

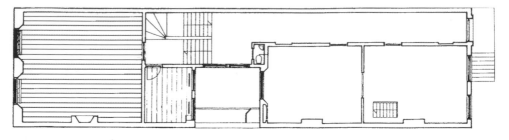

Ground floor plan

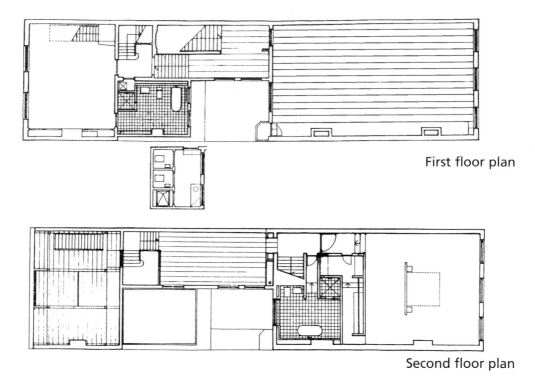

First floor plan

Second floor plan

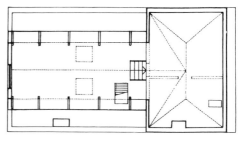

On the right page, several views of the bathroom, where the walls have been covered with small mosaic tiles.

Fourth floor plan

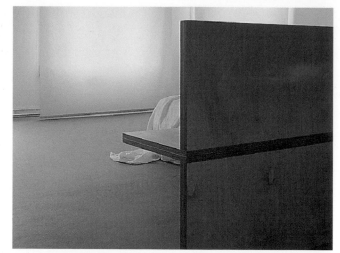

Through the use of roller blinds, the architect minimises the impact of the distribution of openings on the facade and filters the light entering the bedroom.

Camagna Camoletto Marcante
Casa Boggetto
Nice, France

This apartment was devised as a large, comfortable second home in which the 90 sq m of floor space was supplemented by a studio of 30 sq.m. Located in the sixth floor of a building of the fifties in Nice, this dwelling enjoys excellent sea views.

The construction of the interior, in brick, contrasts with the use of fitted cupboards, false walls and drop ceilings, which hide the indirect lighting in the whole apartment. The glass partitions were made using white or transparent Visram 33 and applying 3M films with high-resolution printed images. The fixed or mobile walls, the latter operating as sliding doors, were made in glossy white-painted wood with metal wall systems. The floors were made of white resin with the exception of the bathroom, in which Corian was used. The interior walls and some of the sliding doors were made in glossy white-painted wood with tinted, while the doorknobs and metal frames were made of pol-ished stainless steel. The original layout consisted of a series of fairly narrow rooms, and this scheme aimed to replace it with an open space inspired by the floor plan of a boat. All the technical functions of the dwelling were located in a single block 60 cm wide by 9 m long. This space acts as the backbone of the apartment, in which its rectilinear configuration leads to two rooms at the sides: a habitable space and a corridor. Through a simple system of sliding doors, concealed in the cupboards, a second room for guests with its own bathroom was created. The living-room ends without interruption in a terrace facing the sea that is crossed by a practically invisible wall that allows the views to be extended from the main bedroom. The annexed unit has a bathroom and its own dressing room, separated from the living-room by a giant virtual aquarium. This room can be used as a study or as a guest room thanks to the flexible furniture.

Photographs: Hervè Abbadie

The recurring topic of this scheme is the relationship with the underwater landscape, reproduced through the images of the glass panels that serve as partitions between the spaces.

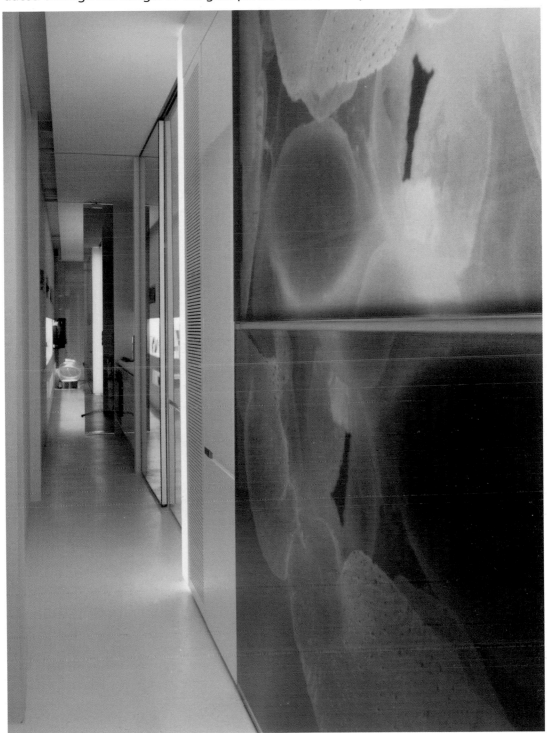

Plan floor

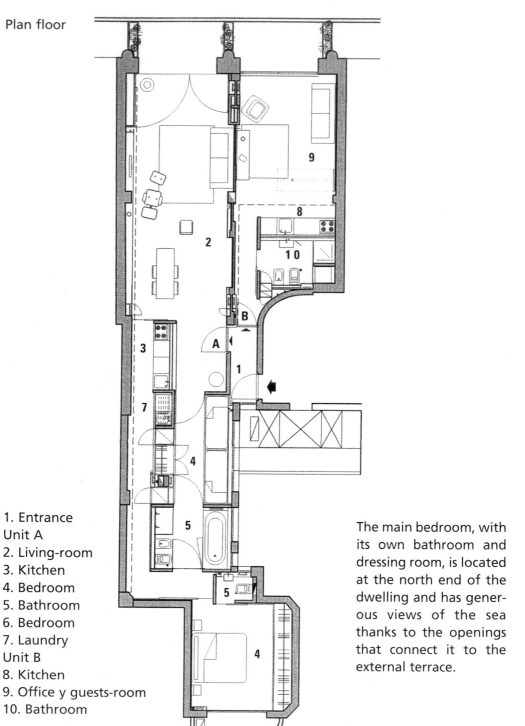

1. Entrance
Unit A
2. Living-room
3. Kitchen
4. Bedroom
5. Bathroom
6. Bedroom
7. Laundry
Unit B
8. Kitchen
9. Office y guests-room
10. Bathroom

The main bedroom, with its own bathroom and dressing room, is located at the north end of the dwelling and has generous views of the sea thanks to the openings that connect it to the external terrace.

Claudio Silvestrin
Thames Apartment
London, UK

The brief was to redesign the interior of a dwelling belonging to the artists Adam and Carolyn Barker-Mill, a space of 250 sq m with one blind wall and three glazed strips. The main factors to be taken into account were the three glazed facades, the presence of thick concrete columns that could not be touched, and the low ceilings.

Leaving the line of the blind wall completely free, Silvestrin arranged the different areas around the three walls giving onto the exterior, thus allowing natural light and views of the city to preside over all the rooms. The landscape and the light seem to flow into the interior, being projected onto the totally white surfaces of the wall and the grey Tuscany stone of the floors. From the entrance hall a gently curving translucent glass screen leads to the living-room and conceals the kitchen. Parallel to this route, a more private route links the bedrooms, kitchen and living-room. The two areas are thus functionally separated but have a certain spatial continuity.

The translucent screen is repeated in the living-room, on the facade facing the river. It acts as a barrier that filters and intensifies the light, creating a dense and evocative atmosphere.

In an exercise of extreme essentiality that is found in all his projects, Silvestrin distributes naked geometrical forms around the dwelling that accentuate the types of material used in each furniture element, from the pear wood benches and tables to the marble piece in which the heating elements are housed, like a clear statement of formal abstraction that results from simplifying function to the maximum, eliminating all secondary elements.

However, a large number of sophisticated details must be solved in order to achieve a naked space such as this: all the functions and facilities are concealed behind glass screens, inside cupboards and walls. This can be seen in the solid white wall that runs longitudinally through the dwelling, housing the light sculptures of Adam Barker-Mill.

Photographs: Tessa Robins

Axonometric view

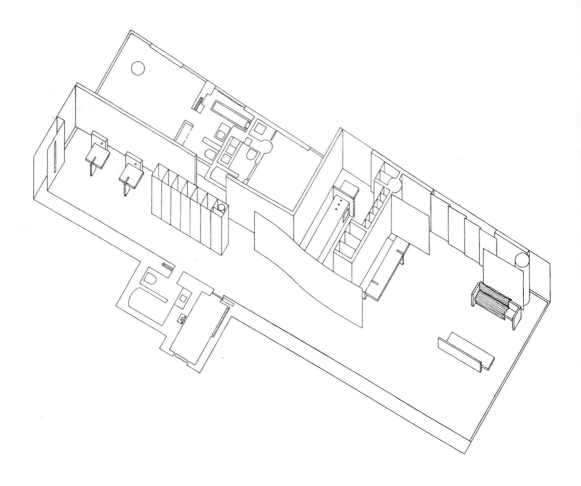

The apartment is arranged around a longitudinal axis that is flanked by a white wall along its whole length.
In the foreground, a view of the curved translucent glass screen that separates the hall from the kitchen and directs us towards the living room in the background.

Floor plan

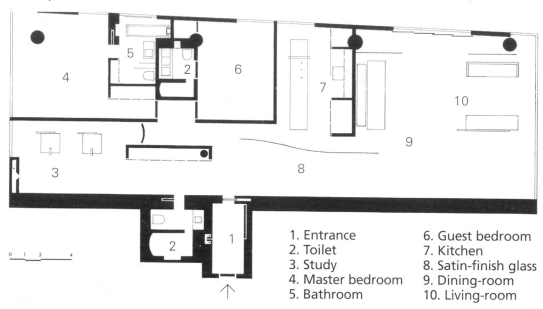

1. Entrance
2. Toilet
3. Study
4. Master bedroom
5. Bathroom
6. Guest bedroom
7. Kitchen
8. Satin-finish glass
9. Dining-room
10. Living-room

Above, detail of the translucent glass panels through which there are marvellous views of the Thames.

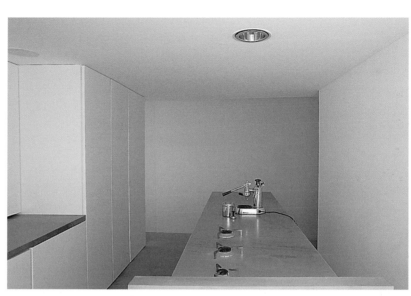

Hiroyuki Arima
House 3R
Fukuoka, Japan

The building is located some distance from the city centre on a site studded with different kinds of trees such us maple and cherry which vary with seasons. The scheme is a conversion of a small old apartment house to provide a favourable environment for living. There is nothing special about the 20-year-old buildings, but a residential pact bans any alterations on the outer appearance. The structures are on a slope running to the north with the front road on the 3r floor level, and access to the maisonette is possible only going underground by stairways from the road level.

"3R" (3 reeds) means three units of a movable wooden wall panel which deployed near the entrance of the maisonette. Since the three units revolve independently of each other, it is possible for a resident to select diverse space variations.

The former interior furnishing in the space have been destroyed and the floors, walls and ceilings are all painted white to make the most of the weak sunlight on the north side. The entire space constitutes a huge continuous structure. Several comers with necessary functions such as the installation area, bedroom, sanitary rooms are deployed continuously in two floors while being connected by a stairwell. The outer walls with the existing sash windows are all covered with translucent plastic panels from inside. Whatever reasonable space there is between the outer walls and the plastic panels is used for a simple storage in each corner, a bar for viewing the greenery or the library. On the face of the wooden panels and plastic panels are certain holes with a variety of diameters. They are used for looking outside or holds for opening and closing the "3R" and door panels, and air ventilation holes of air conditioners.

Photographs: Koji Okamoto

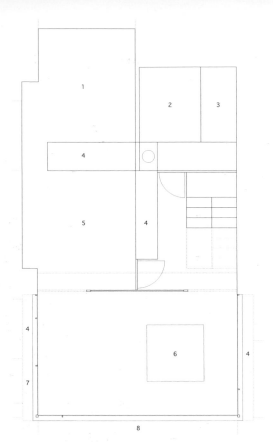

Ground floor plan

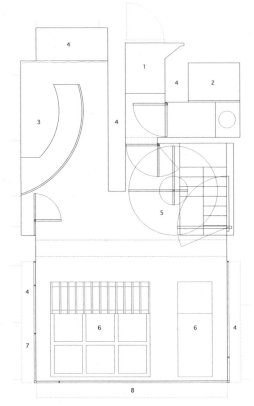

First floor plan

The surfaces that close the apartment, floors, walls and roofs, were painted white in order to reflect and multiply the scarce light from the north that penetrates through the existing openings. These were clad with translucent plastic panels.

A steep slender stairway with a metal skeleton and wooden steps communicates the floor that gives access to the dwelling with the lower level on which most of the private rooms are located.

As can be seen in the photographs, although the two-floor apartment is developed below street level, it takes full advantage of the light coming through the few openings.

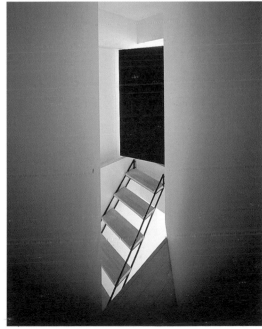

As can be seen in the photographs on this page, the wide range of positions of the three mobile wooden panels provide the owner with a wide variety of spatial combinations.

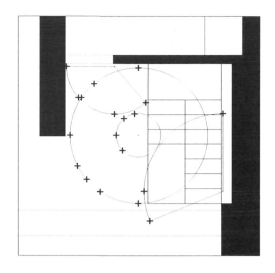
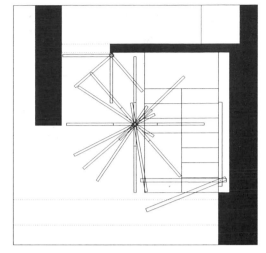

Mobile wooden panels details

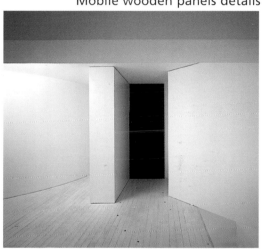

245

Simon Conder
Residencial conversion of a fire station
London, UK

The clients, Andrew Hale the keyboard player and songwriter with Sade, and the cook Stephanie Simon, had bought the top two floors of a redundant Holland Park Fire Station.

Although the buildings was in a quite three lined street, the actual accommodation consisted of a number of small, badly lit rooms with those at the back overshadowed by a mews property only 3.5 metres away from the rear wall.

The depth of the plan was particularly dark. The clients' main objective was to find an imaginative way of transforming this rather depressing environment into a light and exciting new home which would have a generosity of scale and spirit.

At a more detailed level they wanted a solution that would incorporate an open plan living area, the heart of which was to be the kitchen, a large main bedroom with an en-suite bathroom, two smaller bedrooms (one of which was a two double as study). An additional bathroom, and a large amount of built-in storage for clothes and Andrew's large collection of records and compact discs.

The solution developed from an early discussion between Simon Conder and Andrew Hale that took place sitting on the top of the roof. At this level there were dramatic views out over West London and it was clear that the building could be transformed if this rooftop potential could be exploited to create an additional living space and let natural light down in to the centre of the deep plan spaces below.

The final solution was based on three key elements: a roof top conservatory, a flight of stone steps and three-story storage wall. The roof of the conservatory can retract in good weather to create and open roof terrace. This steel and glass structure allows sunlight to flood down into the centre of the second floor living area, and a section of glass floor at this level also allows natural light to penetrate down to the first floor hallway below. The grand flight of tapering stone steps leads directly from the front door street level up to the second floor living area. The storage wall both defines the staircase and separates it from the accommodation at first and second levels.

Photographs: C. Gascoine / VIEW

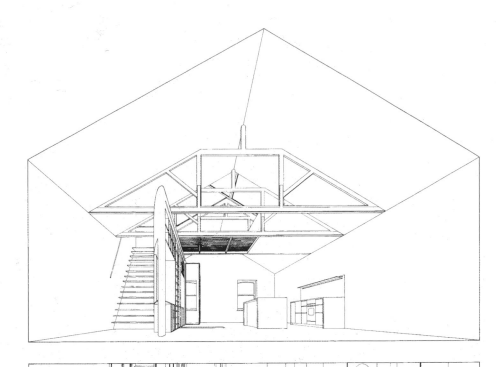

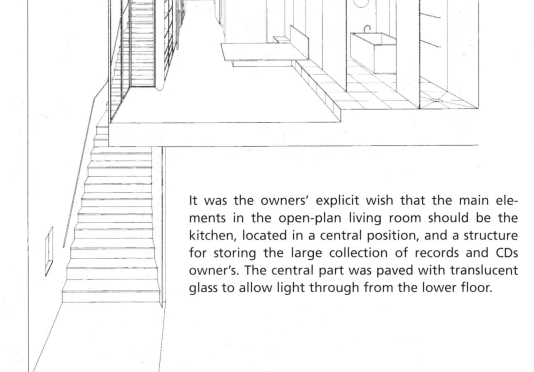

It was the owners' explicit wish that the main elements in the open-plan living room should be the kitchen, located in a central position, and a structure for storing the large collection of records and CDs owner's. The central part was paved with translucent glass to allow light through from the lower floor.

Axonometric view

Views of the bedroom and the main bathroom. The lack of light, a direct consequence of the small size of the openings, was counteracted through the use of light, translucent materials.

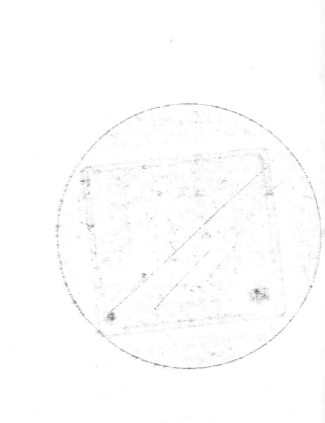